Our Hearts Wonder

Prayers to Heal Your Heart and Calm Your Soul

Our Hearts Wonder

Prayers to Heal Your Heart and Calm Your Soul

S. Renee

Our Hearts Wonder
Prayers to Heal Your Heart and Calm Your Soul

Our Hearts Wonder is a There Is More Inside™ product. There Is More Inside™ is a registered trademark of SRS Productions, Inc.

Publisher:
SRS Productions, Inc.
P.O. Box 177, Dover, DE 19903
www.srenee.com

Special Sales:
There Is More Inside™ books and products are available in special quantity discounts when purchased in bulk by corporations, organizations, special interest groups, and individuals.
Email srenee@srenee.com or call 302-222-4835 for more information.

Cover Design: Wallace King
Editors: Lindsay Wilson and Christina Guthrie
Layout: William McPoyle
Photograph: Jakeem C. Smith

ISBN: 0-9773292-8-3
    1. Spiritual   2. Inspirational   3. Spiritual Growth

Printed in the United States of America
1   2   3 4 5 6 7 8 9 0

Also by S. Renee

There Is More Inside
*Personal Essentials Needed for Living a
Power-Packed Life*

The Bridge to Your Brand
Likability, Marketability, Credibility

Self-Esteem For Dummies
Co-Author
Published by Wiley
Release Date: January 2015

God, we wonder.

Why do people die tragic deaths—car accidents, suicide,
crippling disease, and murder?
Why do young children die before they
have had a chance to live?
Why do family and friends hurt and disappoint us?
Why do we feel powerful one minute and fearful the next?
We wonder, God; our hearts wonder.

Looking unto Jesus the author and finisher of our faith…

Hebrews 12:2a

Foreword by

REVEREND SHIRLEY M. SMITH

Ordained Minister and Mother of the Author

Your sincere prayer is the most powerful force available to you. When you exercise your faith through prayer, the experience will change your life.

I must caution you—you can't depend on what you think, how you feel, or what you can do. It's a faith walk. You have to know within yourself that God will answer. And when you have a moment when you think He won't come through for you, you have to reassure yourself that He loves you enough to deliver an answer.

Your Heavenly Father loves you. He will come through for you with exceptional results that will "blow your natural-born mind." His results are so unexpected and miraculous that you, your friends, and any human being will not be able to explain, pin down, or even guess how they happened.

Through prayer, you can go from ordinary to extraordinary. The accuracy of outcomes as a result of praying is non-changing and dependable. It is the most influential, credible, effective, knowledgeable, powerful, and loyal resource for power, and it guarantees that your life will be transformed.

When you acknowledge God the Father, Jesus the Son, and the Comforter the Holy Spirit and submit to God's will, you find hope, comfort, peace, healing love, forgiveness, grace, mercy, and the fulfillment of your dreams and desires.

My mother instilled the importance of prayer in my life, and I feel blessed to have had the opportunity to pass its importance on to our children.

Growing up, our children heard their father and me praying in our bedroom with the door closed in good and challenging times. We made sure that they took part in the experience of us praying together as a family. Being thankful to God for all His many blessings shown toward others and us was a consistent practice in our home.

Through our actions and words, we taught our children that "prayer is the key to the kingdom and faith unlocks the door." We read the Bible to them so that they would know and understand that "the prayer of a righteous man (woman) is powerful and effective."

We took our children to Sunday school and church. We wanted them to see that "the prayer offered in faith will make the sick person well, the Lord will raise him up" (James 5:15a).

I want to encourage you to talk to Him, and He will talk to you. Here's why:

The reality of the awesomeness of praying manifested itself in S. Renee's life. When she was fired from her job, she was emotionally devastated. Unknowing of what the future would hold for her, she did what she knew to do to create change—she prayed.

After she prayed, without much talk but with plenty of faith, she moved forward with a new attitude, zeal, and direction for her life. This new path was clearly God's purpose.

Since then, through her speaking and media appearances, she has reached millions of people with a message of courage, confidence, and personal leadership. She has authored three self-published books and co-authored a fourth, which is her first book deal.

S. Renee uses prayer as the compass for her life, which is the reason I wanted her to publish some of the prayers she has written for our family.

There are times when you don't know what to say or even how you feel. I hope *Our Hearts Wonder* will give you clarity and support, and provide for you a place to call home.

In God I trust,
Rev. Shirley

Our Hearts Wonder

Prayers to Heal Your Heart and Calm Your Soul

S. Renee

CONTENTS

Section I

Faith

*He says, "Be still, and know that I am God: I will be exalted among the
nations, I will be exalted in the earth. Psalm 46:10*

Section II

Gratitude

*Give thanks in all circumstances; for this is God's will for you in Christ Jesus.
1 Thessalonians 5:18*

Section III

Comfort

So do not fear, for I am with you; do not be dismayed, for I am your God. I will strengthen you and help you; I will uphold you with my righteous right hand. Isaiah 41:10

Section IV

Healing

LORD my God, I called to you for help, and you healed me. Psalm 30:2

Section V

Praise

*Praise the LORD. Give thanks to the LORD, for he is good; his love endures
forever.
Psalm 106:1*

Section VI

A Prayer for You

*"For I know the plans I have for you," declares the LORD, "plans to prosper
you and not to harm you, plans to give you hope and a future." Jeremiah 29:11*

INTRODUCTION

We all have moments when we wonder: Why am I are here? What am I here to do? Why are things happening the way they are? Why is this happening to me?

This book was written to encourage, comfort, and express love toward you, and to remind you that there is a force greater than yourself holding everything—including you.

I believe that prayer is like breathing—it's an unconscious movement of every thought you think, every emotion you feel, and every intention of the words you speak.

Deliberate prayer is like meditation, which is being aware that you are breathing. Deliberate prayer is when you are aware of your thoughts, emotions, and intentions. It's a place of knowing your soul's yearnings and asking God to respond to them.

These prayers were written in a place of consciousness, wonder, gratitude, comfort, and need. They are my words, but you bring them to life. Because I know that we are all one, they are all of *our* souls' desires.

Isn't it your desire to give and receive love? Wouldn't you like to heal from the pain of the loss of a loved one? Don't you have days when uncertainty, fear, and wonder challenge your heart's truth? Aren't there moments when you are in a place of being so blissfully happy that it scares you?

Regardless of how *Our Hearts Wonder* got into your hands, it is with purposeful intention that it landed there. Perhaps you purchased it, it was a gift from a friend, or you found it in an unlikely place. It's in your hands now, Beloved, and God has a plan for how it will serve you.

I like the word "plan," don't you? It means there is a set of actions already in motion. Actions and activities that are beyond your imagination are taking place. All things have already been set up for you; you have to have the courage to walk in it.

That's what prayer offers you—courage. The courage to

believe and do regardless of what you can see, hear, and experience in the present moment. Prayer is your opportunity to sense the presence of divinity from a world that is part of you, yet is beyond you.

In case you have never been told, I want to say it to you now: *"You are special to God. You are unique. You are a spiritual force to be reckoned with. No one in their right mind would even attempt to disturb your meaningful existence."*

I know that situations and circumstances in your life may have caused things to become a little turbulent. These prayers gently and lovingly encourage you to get out of the fight and back into the flow.

God is the author and finisher of *your* faith. Not God's faith in you, but your faith in Him. Your daily communication with God intensifies your faith and changes the texture, dimension, direction, and level of influence of your life.

This doesn't mean you have to be perfect. What it does

mean is that you are willing to be perfected. It means that you are open to seeing and doing things that will improve your life and the lives of others.

God is not complicated. Therefore, He's given you a simple way to communicate with Him. Prayer is letting God know your heart. As you will see in these modest, transparent prayers—it is easy to tell Him your hurts, fears, anxieties, and most importantly, your gratitude, even when you feel like you have nothing to be thankful for.

My friend, I, too, have moments that make me question the hurt, pain, uncertainty, and direction of my life. Moments when my foundation of faith has been shaken. I've found in the midst of my wonder a trust in knowing that all is well.

I am S. Renee, and it is well in the world of wonder!

Section I

FAITH

He says, "Be still, and know that I am God: I will be exalted among the nations, I will be exalted in the earth.

(Psalm 46:10)

FAITH FOR PERSONAL POWER

I doubt you, God. I doubt myself. I doubt everything that I thought I knew to be true. My decisions have led me to the edge, to the end of a path that isn't going anywhere. I am in a place of trouble, defeat, and great distress.

Save me, O God. I don't know where the next step will lead me, but I know I can't do it on my own. I close my eyes to people and situations. I shut down words, thoughts, and voices that are taunting me. I can no longer complain, compare, and compete.

I am suffocating in the clothing of the world. Deceit has worn me out and covered me up. My own ego has drained me of my strength.

In you, God, I seek refuge, comfort, and peace.

You are inside of me. Stand up, O God, within me. I am, and that is enough. And so it is.

In the name of our master, brother, teacher, and friend, Jesus the Christ. Amen.

FAITH TO HAVE FAITH

Through this condition I have learned that my faith is the foundation on which I stand. It's everything that I know to be true. When I surrender my faith, I have nothing.

Heavenly Father, you have my attention. It is through you that I am sustained. You are in every breath that I take, in every movement that I make, and in every thought that I think.

I grant you entry into my heart and mind to influence me. Without shame I acknowledge my darkness with the understanding that you want me to grow without guilt. I, through faith in you and my higher calling, accept the work required for the evolution of my soul.

I ask you, God, that I could somehow see beyond my own selfish desires and cheerfully catch your vision and purpose for the planet—that all people are given the opportunity to prosper and to find and live their highest calling. I am, and so it is.

In the name of our master, brother, teacher, and friend,

Jesus the Christ. Amen.

FAITH IN THE MIDST OF TRAGEDY

Heavenly Father, it is again that my eyes stare down the barrel of tragedy. With a confused mind I wonder why life has delivered to my doorstep this grim earthly conclusion to a sacred soul.

My heart wonders: Did I fail to feel the wind of devastation? Did I not hear the chimes of danger? Did I not see the darkness falling upon me? Or is it simply that my innocence and my lack of knowledge missed the rare signs that led to an abrupt silence?

I can look back and question, or I can look up in faith. There is a purpose in all things. God, you tell me that you're everywhere and in all things. Nothing goes, gets, or squeezes by you.

No man, woman, child, or situation that you possess within your grip can be plucked, pulled, or talked out of your hand. In this I put my trust, faith, and entire being.

Now, as I walk through this valley, I know you are with me. As I grapple with finding the truth, I know that you will light the way. As I seek the peace that passes all understanding, I ask that you remind me that I already possess it. I am, and so it is.

In the name of our master, brother, teacher, and friend, Jesus the Christ. Amen.

FAITH FOR GOOD NEWS

God, before I whisper my first word of the day, I've already felt your presence. For that, I want to say thank you! As I relax in your light and love, I excitedly embrace the day.

I greet your angelic team with a smile to welcome their protection and guidance. I love you, God.

God, let this moment be the focal point of my day. As I interact with others and discover more about myself, in faith I await good news, anticipating a good report.

In the same order, power, and presence that I exist, I declare that all things will come to and through you, as this is the divine order of the universe. I am, and so it is.

In the name of our master, brother, teacher, and friend, Jesus the Christ. Amen.

FAITH TO REACH OTHERS

God, I am excited about my life. I'm not fearful, lacking confidence, or wandering about like a zombie. I am awake, aware, and clear that I have a purpose—thank you.

There are those who do wonder, God. They ponder and are even saddened by what they see. They feel hopeless and misunderstood. At times they question their very existence.

I am a recipient of your love, faithfulness, and healing power. And that which I receive, I am to share.

I pray for them today.

I pray that they may come to know you and experience your joy. If a stranger sees me from afar, let them see the light that you have placed within me. Help them to realize that there is a path leading to abundance.

Should they overhear me in conversation, let the words of my mouth penetrate their heart and move them to a deep level of understanding that you live within them.

Whether they see me from afar or close up, it is my hope, God, that I offer them the faith, a sign, and an answer that reminds them that just as they look up and see the clouds move and give way to the sun, their faith in you will move mountains to give way to their miracle. I am, and so it is.

In the name of our master, brother, teacher, and friend, Jesus the Christ. Amen.

FAITH FOR MERCY AND DIRECTION

God, you have created me to operate powerfully according to the unique gifts and talents that you have placed within me. I thank you for those gifts—the ones that I know I possess and those that I have yet to discover. I realize that what you have given me is powerful. So much so that, at times, I feel overwhelmed, confused, and even scared.

God, I don't always know how to best use these gifts and talents to help others and myself. How can the very things that I possess cause me to run and hide, tremble in fear, and unwillingly destroy myself?

Have mercy, O God. Jesus, have mercy on me.

It is not my conscious choice to choose pain over purpose, drugs over destiny, immorality over morality, poverty over prosperity, sorrow over joy, or ungratefulness over gratitude.

I repent, God, and in this moment, I accept my calling. I

give thanks for my gifts and talents. I know you are with me.

I will now and forevermore, until I depart this planet, stand boldly on the platform of greatness, kindness, and love. I will use all that I have to serve you and mankind. I thank you for your hand of guidance as I courageously walk out of this place of darkness. I am, and so it is.

In the name of our master, brother, teacher, and friend, Jesus the Christ. Amen.

FAITH

Section II

GRATITUDE

Give thanks in all circumstances;
for this is God's will for you in Christ Jesus.
(1 Thessalonians 5:18)

GRATITUDE FOR ANSWERED PRAYER

Glory to the Almighty!

Heavenly Father, I come into your presence with thanksgiving in my heart for the grace that you have extended to me. All things are now in alignment with your will, desire, and grace for my life.

As I am human, it is easy to go back to what I am most familiar. I know that there are many lessons for me to learn. And many ahead that will change the course of my life— developing me into the person you want me to be and leading me to the exact place you have prepared for me.

My heart is open, God. You have my permission to perform according to your will in my life. I need your help.

I ask that you help me to flow with you, even when it doesn't look the way I desire it to look. It is not my intention to resist your will, but if I think that what I'm about to face will hurt, harm, or challenge me, I've learned that I can become fearful and shut down.

I ask that you give me a portion of your wisdom, knowing that it is through your love, wisdom, and peace that I have a foundation to grow and become. I am, and so it is.

In the name of our master, brother, teacher, and friend, Jesus the Christ. Amen.

GRATITUDE FOR THE COURAGE TO TRUST

Father God, in acknowledgement of all that is and forever will be, I am deeply thankful and touched by your generosity towards me.

I feel your presence all around and within me. Inasmuch as your Spirit has risen within me and awakened me to a deeper truth, I know without any hesitation that I am deeply loved by you.

God, it is the love that you share with me that gives me the confidence to love myself and the courage to love others.

Words cannot express my gratitude.

I realize that no matter how hard I try, my behavior can't match the purity of your divinity. No thought that I can think can reach the depth of your understanding. And my heart can't comprehend the totality of the rhythmic mixture of your compassion, forgiveness, and generosity.

Many aspects of your character remain a mystery to me, but I trust you, God. I confess that I don't fully understand what or whom I'm trusting in, but this I know for sure: I'm in good hands, and all is well. I am, and so it is.

In the name of our master, brother, teacher, and friend, Jesus the Christ. Amen.

GRATITUDE FOR PURPOSE

Blessed be the name of the Lord! Heavenly Father, I come before you in this moment as a witness to the magnitude and responsibility you have given me. I feel the heaviness, hurt, and uncertainty of your people, including my own.

As you have preserved my life, I realize that I am a vessel for the accomplishment of your divine will. I ask that you help me and show me how to always seek, possess, and use your divinity and wisdom to take good care of the gifts and talents that you have given me.

I thank you for the discipline to study and the hope to heal.

Glory to you, O God! I am, and so it is.

In the name of our master, brother, teacher, and friend, Jesus the Christ. Amen.

GRATITUDE IN THE MIDST OF PAIN

God, I know that you are holding my aching heart and troubled soul. I worship you, God, and give thanks to you for what I'm experiencing. You know my heart. It has been difficult to understand and deal with this.

My heart wonders: Have I done something wrong? What did I do to deserve this? Will it ever get better?

God, I stand on your word. I put my entire being in your hands. I trust that this is to purify my faith, make me stronger, and increase my understanding.

My weaknesses are exposed. I surrender to you, O God. Make me wiser and show me how to create more space in my heart for greater compassion for others. Let this not be in vain.

Thank you for your love and comfort. I love you, God. I am, and so it is.

In the name of our master, brother, teacher, and friend, Jesus the Christ. Amen

GRATITUDE FOR FAMILY AND FRIENDS

God, thank you for your impression on my soul that identifies me as belonging to you. I'm thankful for my protective and guiding angels who behold your face. I'm grateful for my family and friends whom you appointed to my life before the foundation of the world.

It is a gift to have the opportunity to travel through life with them. When I sense their presence and see their familiar faces, I have the feeling of joy and safety. I'm reminded that I am not alone.

I know that they are my teachers, and I am theirs. Their gift to me is the opportunity to learn and grow. My gift to you is to share the love and lessons with others.

Thank you for a heavenly plan that gives me a feeling of connection and love while on earth. I am, and so it is.

In the name of our master, teacher, brother, and friend, Jesus the Christ. Amen.

GRATITUDE FOR ANOTHER DAY

I give thanks to you, O God, for your tender mercies, which are renewed each day. I thank you for allowing me to breathe with you and through you. I consider it a privilege to open my heart and mouth to give praise unto you. I honor you and all your wondrous works. I am, and so it is.

In the name of our master, brother, teacher, and friend, Jesus the Christ. Amen.

GRATITUDE FOR THE CLOSE OF A DAY

As the day comes to an end, I shall not forget to say, "Lord, thank you for the miracles I've been blessed to witness today."

I thank you for what my eyes have seen and my ears have heard, as these things serve as reminders that I need you today, always, and in all ways.

It's a humbling place to enter into your presence in the awareness that you know everything—before, during, and after it happens.

Before I utter a word, you know my heart. Before I extend my hand, you know my intention, and before my soul yearns, you know my desire.

I am in deep gratitude for faith, favor, and fortitude that assists me as I continue on my journey. Thank you for bringing back to my remembrance the significance of a heart and mind that looks to you always. I am, and so it is.

In the name of our master, brother, teacher, and friend, Jesus the Christ. Amen.

Section III

COMFORT

So do not fear, for I am with you; do not be dismayed, for I am your God. I will strengthen you and help you; I will uphold you with my righteous right hand.

(Isaiah 41:10)

COMFORT OF ACCEPTANCE

I come to adore you, Christ the Lord.

Heavenly Father, I enter into your presence humbled by your love and gift of acceptance. With every fiber of my being as I inhale and take in the breath of life, I smile at you and say, "To you, O God, be the glory."

I'm so grateful that I don't have to pretend to be smart or kind or successful, or even important.

In your presence, I don't have to struggle to move or speak in any particular way to get your attention. When I close my eyes and give you my attention, your acceptance engulfs me. In this divine space, I can be myself without thought. This is freedom.

God, I know that you have no expectation of me but to be your wonderfully magnificent creation. With my entire being I desire that God. But I don't know what that means. I don't know what it feels like to embrace my entire essence that is you. How can I reach that level of wholeness? I want to be complete and connected to you, God.

I can only do that which I know. Teach me to be silent. Show me how to be whole. Allow me to see the space that has been created for me to just be. Right now, I release myself to you. I am, and so it is.

In the name of our master, brother, teacher, and friend, Jesus the Christ. Amen.

COMFORT FOR LOSS

God, the silence has come. My family and friends have gone on with their lives. I am left to walk this path alone. I am hurting. I am weak. My heart has stopped beating. The pain is unbearable.

No one can see the spear lodged in my heart. No one can tell that I'm bleeding. I feel left alone to die.

God, why can't anyone see that I'm buried in hurt and anger? Why can't anyone hear my scream for help?

I don't want to continue. My own thoughts scare me. I cry for my own death.

I am petitioning you, God, for strength. I seek your presence. I need a way out of darkness. Where is your light, O God?

Remind me of how deeply loved I am by you. I need a sign that you exist. I need you, God. Please, show yourself to be true. I depend on your answer to this prayer. I am, and so it is.

In the name of our master, brother, teacher, and friend, Jesus the Christ. Amen.

COMFORT FOR CONNECTION

*Another day to look within and find you, O God, nestled in
my soul and divinely connected through your Spirit.
Thank you for your everlasting presence, guidance,
forgiveness, and support. I am open to your direction as I
begin my day.*

*I ask that you nudge me to always speak with care, listen
with intention, and move as a purposeful disciple of my
master, brother, teacher, and friend, Jesus the Christ. I am,
and so it is. Amen.*

Section IV

HEALING

O Lord my God, I cried unto thee,

and thou hast healed me.

(Psalm 30:2)

HEALING FROM SELF-NEGLECT

Heavenly Father, through the grace and mercy of my Lord and Savior, Jesus the Christ, I enter into your presence with thanksgiving. Regardless of what I may think or feel in judgment of others and myself, it is your divine will that I stand in this space and in my current condition.

For this reason I celebrate this time of challenge that has been created to shift me in my thinking and create a greater awareness of where I am—and, more importantly, where I need to be.

I relinquish judgment and resistance to what is. I celebrate this opportunity to embrace the abundance of your love, peace, and understanding. God, you accept me as I am because you can see my brilliance, even when I'm in the midst of darkness.

You said, "Ask, and it shall be given," not because you needed to know my desires, but because I need to know my desires. And so now, God, I ask for mental, emotional, spiritual, physiological, and psychological healing and cleansing.

I seek clarity and direction. I ask that you help me move out of the danger zone and into alignment with you and who I really am.

I give thanks for this journey. It continuously allows me to make my way back home—back home to you, Lord, and to myself.

I recognize that I have everything that I need. You have blessed me with so much. Abundance is all around me and within me.

As I confess that I have abandoned myself, please forgive me. I know that it is done. God, teach me how to release myself from the prison of unforgiveness toward myself and others.

Being called to serve on this planet is an honor. I recognize, God, that it is an honor. And it is my intention to fulfill my calling. Through the power and authority of your Word, I am blessed and know that there is a divine and joyous plan for my life. I am, and so it is.

In the name of our master, brother, teacher, and friend, Jesus the Christ. Amen.

HEALING FROM PAST MISTAKES

God, my soul is in agony. My choices condemn me. The guilt and shame of my actions entangle my soul with torment. I am choking on my own misery.

I want to make my way back to you, God. But I don't know how.

I know that in your presence, my eyes will behold the light of beauty and truth. Your Spirit will transform my words, which will transcend barriers of hopelessness. And my soul will be rescued from self-inflicted poison.

God, my heart is open. You are welcome in this space. It is now that I sit down so that you can stand up. I am humbled by your presence. I am, and so it is.

In the name of our master, brother, teacher, and friend, Jesus the Christ. Amen.

HEALING FOR A SICK LOVED ONE

Heavenly Father, my faith serves as a witness, and every miraculous sign that I have seen serves as evidence that you hear me and will answer according to your will and plan for my life. I want to thank you for access to your kingdom and great glory.

God, I've watched the suffering of my loved one, and it grieves me. Not only because of the pain, but because I've failed to have the compassion to see, understand, and comprehend the magnitude of what they have to bear— forgive me.

Father God, you are great in grace and mercy. Your work never ceases to amaze the mind of man. You said in your Word to make all requests known unto you. I'm asking you to comfort and to ease the pain. Create a divine barrier between them and the pain while you heal their body and calm their soul.

And God, may your divine support and answer to this

prayer show all of us the value of residing in a safe place with you.

I thank you for yet another miracle. I am, and so it is.

In the name of our brother, master, teacher, and friend, Jesus the Christ. Amen.

HEALING FROM JUDGMENT

Gracious Father, I humbly come into your presence with thanksgiving in my heart. I am thankful for your loving and forgiving nature. You don't judge us, yet we constantly judge ourselves and one another.

Forgive me for those moments when I judge. I confess that I don't really know what a person is feeling and thinking. Neither do I know what they have experienced in life that makes them behave the way they do.

Your Word reminds me of this fatal crime against your kingdom—renew me and teach me what it truly means to be one with you and a friend to them. I am, and so it is.

In the name of our master, brother, teacher, and friend, Jesus the Christ. Amen.

Section V

PRAISE

Praise the Lord! Oh, give thanks to the Lord, for He is good!

For His mercy endures forever.

(Psalm 106:1)

PRAISE FOR EMPOWERMENT

Heavenly Father, I give thanks to you. I am empowered by your presence. It is through you that I courageously embrace my day and every assignment that shall come forth.

My ears are open to your truth, my eyes are prepared to see your beauty, and my heart is ready to offer your love and compassion.

I praise you, O God, because it is only through you that I can offer this planet and others such an awesome gift.

Being in this place of peace means wanting nothing. I am, and so it is.

In the name of our master, brother, teacher, and friend, Jesus the Christ. Amen.

PRAISE FOR HEALING

God, I am thankful to see this day come, as your will is done—total recovery has been granted. Your hand and heart are with me. Your presence surrounds me. Your wisdom guides me.

Heavenly Father, I rejoice because of you. It is good to know your love, protection, and miraculous power. I pause to ask: What do you want me to learn? How do you want me to change? What would you like for me to do?

As I meditate on these questions today, I ask that your angels of light minister to my heart so that I may uncover the mysteries of your truth. I am, and so it is.

In the name of our master, brother, teacher, and friend, Jesus the Christ. Amen.

PRAISE FOR MERCY

I give thanks to you, O God, for what continues to be a journey of lessons and blessings. It is always your practice to have mercy on your people. I am thankful for your mercy because I know, see, hear, and live with my mistakes, imperfections, and, at times, awful behavior.

I know that I should continue to seek and open myself up to you. By doing so, I learn, grow, and evolve into a loyal, trusted follower of my master, brother, teacher, and friend, Jesus the Christ. I am, and so it is. Amen.

PRAISE FOR FAITHFULNESS

God, you have been my confidence since my youth. In you and your unfailing love do I put my trust. I, through my faith in you only, send angels of light and love to my family to support them as they carefully navigate through life.

Thank you for every signpost that signifies your presence in their lives. Thank you for your protection, and for fulfillment of their lives' purposes. As they continue on this journey, let them be a beam of brilliant light on planet earth. I am, and so it is.

In the name of our master, brother, teacher, and friend, Jesus the Christ. Amen.

PRAISE FOR POWER

Heavenly Father, I am humbled by your mightiness and power. I'm engulfed in the vastness of your being. Although your divinity is spacious, I feel safe as I float and flow in it. This is a perfect place to be—feeling loved and lovable, free and open, creative and unlimited.

My heart refuses all trouble and seeks only your infinite wisdom and answers.

As I return to myself, filled with your Spirit and with light and love, I am ready to do the work. I am, and so it is.

In the name of our master, brother, teacher, and friend, Jesus the Christ. Amen.

Section VI

A PRAYER FOR YOU

"For I know the plans I have for you," declares the LORD,
"plans to prosper you and not to harm you,
plans to give you hope and a future."

(Jeremiah 29:11)

A PRAYER FOR YOU, THE READER

*God, thank you for this person whose hands Our Heart
Wonders has entered and whose heart it has touched. Bless
them God.*

*As I know that their eyes have not seen and ears have not
heard, nor has it entered into their heart all of what you
have for them, I ask that you grant them their heart's wish
and soul's desire according to your will.*

*Surround them Lord. Let no harm come close to their
doorstep or that of their loved ones. Let sin avenge not, but
let your grace and mercy reign gloriously in their life so
that they will find their rightful and righteous place in you.*

*Let joy be their home and peace be their residence. I pray,
Lord, that your light and love will shine within and around
them.*

*I declare by your Word that they will live on and with
purpose. That no good thing will be withheld from them,*

they will lead and not follow, and everything that you have started to create in and with them will be accomplished.

I affirm over their life that all that you have purposed for them and generations to come will be fulfilled on earth as it has been completed in heaven. And so it is.

In the name of our master, brother, teacher, and friend, Jesus the Christ. I love you. Amen.

"I am the Alpha and the Omega," says the Lord God,

"who is, and who was, and who is to come, the Almighty."

(Revelation 1:8)

Other Books By S. Renee

S. Renee is author of *There Is More Inside* and *The Bridge to Your Brand*. She is co-author of *Self-Esteem For Dummies (Wiley)*, which will release nationally January 2015.

There Is More Inside helps readers develop the courage and confidence to live their life on purpose. S. Renee shares her uncertain journey of questioning her life's purpose to the fulfillment of her life dream of becoming a model and television talk show host.

She also opens up about being fired from her job, being diagnosed as being depressed and finding a deeper relationship with God in the midst of darkness. *There Is More Inside* shows you how to reclaim your life.

The Bridge to Your Brand teaches readers how to be likable, marketable, and credible by developing a personal brand. S. Renee developed a personal brand model using the life of Jesus Christ, who continues to have the most influential, reliable personal brand of anyone who has ever walked on planet earth.

She teaches her God-inspired model to employees, entrepreneurs, pastors, and people like you.

Self-Esteem For Dummies helps readers learn how to break free of negative self-concepts and self-defeating behavior, build healthy new relationships or strengthen those they have, dissolve internal barriers to success in work and love, become better leaders by helping others improve their self-esteem, breakthrough the fear that is zapping their faith, and nurture self-esteem in children.

About the Author

S. Renee's expertise in personal, professional, and spiritual development is highly sought after by Fortune 500 corporations, colleges and universities, government and non-profit agencies, and faith-based communities. She is highly praised for her self-development programs and innate ability to create shifts in people's thinking and inspire them to take steps toward positive, permanent change.

S. Renee is endorsed by and shares platforms with well-known international speakers and leaders, such as *Chicken Soup for the Soul* originator Jack Canfield; ABC journalist and author of *Step Out on Nothing* Byron Pitts; and fourth-season winner of *The Apprentice,* entrepreneur and author of *Campus CEO* Dr. Randal Pinkett.

With 20 years of self and public image development experience, she is an expert in self-esteem development and an image consultant, motivational speaker, and life and branding coach. She is an expert resource to regional and national media outlets.

S. Renee is Honorary Commander of the Department of Defense Charles C. Carson Center for Mortuary Affairs—the only mortuary for dignified transfer of fallen United States soldiers. She serves on the United Way of Delaware Women in Leadership Council and the Commission on Early Education and the Economy. She's a Commissioner on the Human Relations Commission for the City of Dover, and she serves on the Delaware Community Foundation Kent County Advisory Board—Delaware's largest philanthropic organization. She is also chair of the William J. and Rev. Shirley M. Smith, Sr. Scholarship Fund.

A former QVC model, television talk-show host and spokesperson in Philadelphia, and director of public relations, she has also worked for Fortune 500 companies in marketing and management. Learn more about S. Renee at www.srenee.com.

www.ingramcontent.com/pod-product-compliance
Lightning Source LLC
Chambersburg PA
CBHW071831020426
42331CB00007B/1683